I Used to Remember the Story of How

poems by

Katherine E. Schneider

Finishing Line Press
Georgetown, Kentucky

I Used to Remember
the Story of How

Copyright © 2019 by Katherine E. Schneider
ISBN 978-1-64662-092-0 First Edition
All rights reserved under International and Pan-American Copyright Conventions. No part of this book may be reproduced in any manner whatsoever without written permission from the publisher, except in the case of brief quotations embodied in critical articles and reviews.

ACKNOWLEDGMENTS

Ruminate: "Lantern"
The Poetry Porch: "Sightings"

I'd like to express my heartfelt gratitude to all who participated in inspiring, encouraging, workshopping, and advising upon the work contained here. May you know how valued you are.

Dr. Kim Bridgford, once my college professor, then my MFA mentor, now my manuscript reviewer, and ever a supporter of my writing and development—I thank you more than I can say.

Baron Wormser, many thanks to you. Your wisdom and guidance during your work with me have reverberated strongly here and in the rest of my life.

My Fairfield University MFA colleagues, mentors, and friends, you occupy a special place in my heart and have fed and nurtured much of what is here. Thank you.

And finally, thank you to all those people in my life who have nourished and blessed my spirit and helped me to keep holding up my lantern—
to my family, my dear friends, my teacher colleagues, and my former students.

Publisher: Leah Maines

Editor: Christen Kincaid

Cover Art and Design: Katherine E. Schneider

Author Photo: Katherine E. Schneider

Printed in the USA on acid-free paper.
Order online: www.finishinglinepress.com
     also available on amazon.com

Author inquiries and mail orders:
Finishing Line Press
P. O. Box 1626
Georgetown, Kentucky 40324
U. S. A.

Table of Contents

Say Go, 1

Breath, 2

Beatitudes, 4

The Conviction of Things Not Seen, 6

Unwelcome, 8

Jesus Wept, 9

Small Stray Rocks, 11

Silent Inhale, 13

Scent of Cedar, 14

Hold in Your Mind, 15

Dock, 16

Midtown West, 17

Mirage, 19

Some Tinder, 20

Thirty Pieces of Silver, 21

Untitled, 22

You Knew, I Knew, 23

The Send-off, 24

Sightings, 25

Noah, 26

Old King David, 27

Disciple, 28

Lantern, 30

I Used to Remember the Story of How, 32

I Will Be With You Always, 33

*To all the precious people who have loved me,
most especially my mother and father.
This love is forever.*

SAY GO

go to the place where you start again and say go
start again at the question you've already asked
start from a place you've been to before
and listen to the GPS say *continue on*

go to the place where your grandmother rests
remembering you, forgetting everything else
start from a place you both will remember
and listen to the GPS say *continue on*

go take a drive in the sunshine in the autumn
start again on heights of hope you couldn't forget
mindful enough now in the present to cherish it
and listen to the GPS say *continue on*

BREATH

When I sit beside you in church,
I can hear you breathe,

I rarely think of you so mortally.

I can feel you lean back in the pew,
can feel the creaking wood against

your push—
your shoulder muscle and bone,

can feel the vibration of
your anxious foot.

If I glance over I can see
the profile of your face—

long nose, brown eye,
angle of jaw line,

your still and placid gaze,
dark hair falling beside.

When we stand and sing,
I can hear your voice

sound with mine.
Eyes close, hands lift—a moment sublime.

Hands fall, eyes open—
rapture subsides.

The benediction is said;
we move to leave.

We stretch our arms; we yawn and blink.

Did you forget?
>	You and I are finite things

>	depending
on a breath.

BEATITUDES

The discouraged people
                        are blessed
The grieving people
                        are blessed
The gentle people
                        are blessed
The protestors
                        are blessed
The merciful people
                        are blessed
The innocent people
                        are blessed
The people who make peace
                        are blessed
The people who suffer
for the good things they believe
                        are blessed

They
        will have heaven
They
        will receive comfort
They
        will own the Earth
They
        will get justice
They
        will experience mercy
They
        will see God
They
        will represent God
They
        will have heaven

The discouraged people
The grieving people
The gentle people
The protestors
The merciful people
The innocent people
The people who make peace
The people who suffer
for the good things they believe

                        are blessed
                        are blessed
                        are blessed
                        are blessed
                        are blessed
                        are blessed
                        are blessed
                        are blessed

They
They
They
They
They
They
They
They

        will have heaven
        will receive comfort
        will own the Earth
        will get justice
        will experience mercy
        will see God
        will represent God
        will have heaven.

THE CONVICTION OF THINGS NOT SEEN

> *When John [the Baptist] heard in prison what Christ was doing, he sent his disciples to ask him, "Are you the one who was to come, or should we expect someone else?" -Matthew 11:2-3*

I
The sun's steady gaze burned your back all day,
yet you were unconcerned with your garments—
addicted, consumed by the mission.

Even in the womb you kicked for it.

There was nothing to distract. Nothing
to complicate the life that existed
to clamor and cry—

make ready.

For this one purpose you called from the Jordan,
wading through water, beckoning
the conscience-stricken, dunking them under
and lifting them again, again.

No appetite overwhelmed the hunger of preparation;
nothing could compete with the exhilaration of imminence,

a holy rescue at hand,

your steady gaze
fixed on the Kingdom of Heaven.

II
At last you beheld the King, whom you baptized,
and over whom the voice of God spoke
in thundering glory through the daylight.

It must have been thrilling, almost unbelievable.

At that moment how did you not
erupt in celebration?
How did you not jump and splash
and kick at the water?

How did you not wade out
to the bank and follow Him;
perch yourself on a shady hill
and contemplate your wonder?

There were still many
who needed to hear you calling out;
this was your calling—

to never stop working, preparing the way.

Matthew says that even before dying,
you had to be sure.

UNWELCOME

> *"They got up, drove him out of the town, and took him to the brow of the hill on which the town was built, in order to throw him down the cliff." -Luke 4:28-29*

In Your own town they drove You
        to the edge of a cliff—

those; first delighted, then enraged,
        now poised to kill—

They rose up offended
        at what You had said.

When two prophets were rejected,
        they helped gentiles instead.

Implying that You would do the same,
        it turned the Nazarene's pride to hate.

But it was not Your time to die—
        You escaped through the mob,

jostling the thick shoulders of those
        You meant to save,

those who grew up beside You,
        those You made from dry dust.

And we have never stopped doing this;
        driving You to the edge of a cliff,

angry with what You've said.
        We fully intend to push you off,

to hear You break like a fable below—
        and be our own gods instead.

JESUS WEPT

I
When I read the text, it seemed
that grief was unexpected.

All the way to Bethany, two days late,
you explained that Lazarus would awaken,
that he was only asleep,

his illness a cause
for a display of God's glory.

It seemed the disciples made you numb
by their constant misunderstanding;
they didn't comprehend until you said it plainly—

you knew that Lazarus was already dead.

II
You reassured Martha when
she met you on the road and when she stated
a faith so clear—

she knew you were the Christ—
believed you would raise the dead.

You knew what you were about to do,

but as you walked calmly, nearer
to the tomb, a crowd of mourners
and Mary ran out to you.

She fell at your feet as the others
were still coming, and you saw

that all of them were crying.

Perhaps it struck you in that moment—
you, as much God as man—

the stunning loss of death.

III
Mary uttered faith and an indictment:
Lord, if you had been here, my brother

would not have died.

A sudden groaning in your spirit
hushed instruction—
Lazarus, but a stitch in the tapestry of man.

Lazarus, your friend.

All you managed to ask was,
Where have you laid him?

                                        before you wept.

SMALL STRAY ROCKS

I sit at the edge of the Sound
as white light sings out
between broad strokes
of cloud.

My friend,
he's skipping stones,
I watch them jump
across the current—

leaping at first,
just tapping the surface,
then hopping splashes,
before sinking.

His hands are thick
and rivered with veins,
gripping rocks
and launching them.

His hands gently comb
the hard, smooth shore
for small stray rocks
like words—

so particular about them,
selecting only certain ones
of the few
he finds—

to believe they will
go far before sinking

after leaving his palm
where they are waiting,

so solid and cool
he could almost feel
and taste them
on his articulate tongue.

SILENT INHALE

The trees behind the lake
are the black veins

and orange and yellow leaves
are the illuminated flesh

of the monarch's wing—
segmented stained glass.

I want to be there and see
the path between the trees—

each bowing breath and tilt
of wing.

SCENT OF CEDAR

You broke and twisted free
a stick from a thin, dead cedar.

You showed me the rosy marrow
revealed at the breaking place.

I bent close and breathed
the thick, cologne aroma

and looked up to wonder
what was hidden in your face.

HOLD IN YOUR MIND

the tiny violet that grows
in the soil
of your chest—

a twisting prayer
watered by tears
coaxed

by the beat that remains there.

Gather around it
fragments—
the glass tones of a song—

a song for the heavens to hear
sung as echoes between your ears.

DOCK

There's a slow rhythm to the waves
and it will never stop.
Someone else should be here to see
the red fading of the sun,
all these docked boats lined up.
I want someone beside me,
a voyeur friend to nod as I point—

to see the blush sunset and the boats
and maybe know something about me.

MIDTOWN WEST

Stone benches
have overtaken
half of Broadway
along
with wire tables and chairs.

The white face
of the sun warms them
though it is
still winter here.

I attempt to relax,
seated on stone,
beside traffic,
small journal held close
to me.

I'm afraid
someone will see
what I've written in pen—
the hope that hurts:

that you will answer me

before I become
a stranger again,
before I cut
my hair again,
before I give in to silence.

This is something
I would tell you:
they've even painted
the pavement green,

and the stranger thing—
that I've grown used to this—

used to sitting
in the street,

used to sifting myself
into and out of

this fickle, transforming city.

MIRAGE

I often picture you—
your dark hair against
the summer afternoon sun
as you're carrying a ladder
or planks of wood—
and how some of your curls
disappear in the light
and shine, halo-like.

In some New England neighborhood
you'll be demolishing with sledges—
smashing rotted walls,
or building with snarling drills
and the precise thwack of nails.

But when you take a break,
walking away from the sawdust,
with sweat and sunburn
on your cheeks, you think
of what you really want to do:
to put musician fingers
to guitar strings,
be paid the rest of your life
to sing.

Your stare is a stare of destiny,
fixed on the horizon line
of pavement swimming with heat.
It pierces through
to a cool, evening venue
where dim lights and blues melodies,
set your mind at ease—
where, smiling, you'll look
in my direction

to the place where our eyes
nearly meet.

SOME TINDER

Instead of ripping open a bag of exclamations,
you walk out from behind the counter
and open your arms with your squint-eyed smile.

Without a word from me, you pull me
to your solid chest, without even knowing this
was my wish—encircling affection, borrowed warmth.

You tilt your head down, press your cheek
to my hair, and just a little tighter you squeeze—

but really, I'm only your customer—

chilled by the draft from the opening door,
prone to a skin of frost.

THIRTY PIECES OF SILVER

A crash in the sanctuary—
silver splayed on the floor,
thrown from the hand of Judas—
echoing, rattling on the stone.

But even after, Judas felt
as if it had never left his hand;
he felt it slipping, cold in his palm,
then winding up around his arm—

a serpent he could not drop
a weight he could not throw.

UNTITLED

We are pulled into the undertow of crowds
before we even begin.

Just as soon as I've let my eyes
linger on your face,
conceive of wanting you
to stay,
you must catch your train—
you look toward the track.

We are already closing ourselves,
becoming vague, as you walk away.

YOU KNEW, I KNEW

Your voice wasn't perfect;
you were never all in-tune.

But when you sang,
whenever you sang—
I always listened to you.

Your thin hair flew in the beach breeze;
it flattened to your head in the rain.

You didn't look at me,
but I looked at you—
and you knew, I knew.

I didn't trust unspoken things.
I didn't believe what they could say.

Wordlessly, I loved you then.
And wordlessly
It washed away.

THE SEND-OFF

The afterwarmth of goodbye hugs
numbed me just long enough
to let you go.

The sun was hot,
you saw me off
waving and squinting
from the curved sidewalk.

I guess I can say I felt safe in your love,
in leaving something full.

I've replayed this film strip many times.
Since you died, it reminds me
how bright,
how full.

SIGHTINGS

Gloaming: when the trees are black, when
the horizon glows purple, emerald, blue,
I imagine that you are beckoning at the edge
of the forest—a whisper I want to believe.

I take it home with me, lay my head to pillow—
more likely you will appear in dreams;
leaving your dorm room and locking the door,
or waving from a crawl space high up on the wall.

I felt a resonant presence, a late warmth
that hovered, a teasing comfort after you had died.
It lingered—for years, for longer than I knew you—
in a young man's soft voice and brush of auburn hair.

If nowhere else, I can still glimpse you there.

NOAH

                                      I liked you before I knew you

I love your steadiness,
your name means rest.

                                      when I met you with
                                      your long brown hair

I love your clarity,
the sharp way you see things.

                                      to sign you up on cello
                                      in the college orchestra.

I love your joy:
the wild blackberries you find.

                                      That first autumn when
                                      you left sheet music behind,

I love your knowledge,
how you can name the trees.

                                      I recognized it before
                                      I turned off the stage lights,

I love the way you see a problem
and start measuring and building.

                                      and after I put my bass away
                                      in the pouring rain,

I love each year you've grown
in kindness towards me.

                                      I brought it to you to be
                                    the one who brought it to you,

Despite your preferred seclusion,
you made room for me

                        though it was unnecessary.

OLD KING DAVID

As an old man King David curled upon
his bed, but blankets could not keep him warm.
Unused to peace, the weakness in his arms
unsettled him when anxious dreams would come.
For though the wrath of jealous Saul was gone,
and enemies defeated with the threats
of traitorship at home upon the death
of Absalom—so much had come to harm.

Perhaps in those last days he smiled to think
of purer things untainted and unspoiled—
of writing songs to God who gave him rest,
of Jonathan, dear friend of youth—to dream
of afternoons as just a shepherd boy.
Perhaps these glowing embers warmed him best.

DISCIPLE

> "'My prayer is not for them alone. I pray also for those
> who will believe in me through their message'" —John 17:20
>
> "When he had finished praying, Jesus left with his disciples
> and crossed the Kidron Valley." —John 18:1

Our rabbi spoke to us as if
his words might be the last we'd hear.

We still could hardly understand
what his message meant, but then,

we followed him, as we always did,
toward the grove of olives.

Through the Kidron Valley we walked;
quiet as the dark blue night

settling in across the sky, he led the way:
I saw his back but not his eyes.

Some clouds caught one last flame
of sun, an edge in pink and orange,

revealed anew as we moved over hills,
passing ancient graves whose dead might be

the dust on our feet, mingled
in the footsteps of great King David

as we followed *our* son of David—

was this fulfilled prophecy
or a dream?

Before this walk in twilight glow,
he prayed for us in Jerusalem.

Though sated from supper we looked up
at his voice and, watching his face,

it made us wonder. He prayed
for those who would believe

when we would tell them the things
we'd seen and known. But how far

could we go? On foot, we now
are ordinary men at fall of night,

dark bodies in the fading light.

LANTERN

Suddenly all I see
is the lantern in my hand;
assaulted by rain,
its flame alive.

Midnight came fast,
and darkness edged in
between the trees,
across the leaf-layered ground,

and left me lost.

I remember the evening,
how the sunset
flashed on my eyes
like an old filmstrip;

bright and silent,
light as breath, and ancient,
etched onto my memory.
Hypnotized,

I fell asleep.

Later, when the storms rolled in,
they washed those watercolors away—
bled every image wet and heavy,

and woke me in a flood of gray.

I almost drowned for shock and sadness
until I lifted up my arm;
and I could see the step before me,

and the next one after that.

I must move to be rescued,
to find a way beyond this place.

The flame defies the dark,
and I see I am not alone;
there are others waking in the night,
and lifting their lanterns,

walking home.

I USED TO REMEMBER THE STORY OF HOW

Salvation met you like snow
in the cold canyon of a stadium.
It melted on your fevered face
and praise steamed from your skin—you sang.

I close my eyes and I can see you
running up those lighted stairs;

I see you falling on your knees,
spreading your arms and waiting—

for whatever would fall
from the sky;

whether bread,

or starlight—

I WILL BE WITH YOU ALWAYS

Look, I said,
I will be with you.
Always.

Until the world
we know
melts away.

In every moment,
when you know,
and when you don't.

From now
until
the deafening light—

even if you don't see me—
you'll be in me,
behind my eyes.

Look, I said,
I will be here
even if you are not—

this promise
is every particle,
every wave.

It binds us
across oceans
of difference and pain.

Look, I said,
This love is forever.
And it is with you.

And I am with you.
Always.

Katherine E. Schneider is a teacher and poet residing in Norwalk, Connecticut. She grew up in Somers, New York, with a loving and supportive family and art, music, and English teachers who encouraged her. After that, she attended Fairfield University for her Bachelor of Arts and was part of the inaugural cohort of Fairfield University's Master of Fine Arts in Writing degree where she worked closely with Kim Bridgford and Baron Wormser. She also completed a Master of Arts in TESOL degree from University of Southern California which enabled her to transition from work in publishing to work in the world of teaching and advocating for adult ESL students. For the past seven years she has been teaching English language to adult international students and immigrants who delight and inspire her every day.

Katherine E. Schneider contributed the essay on Kassia to The Mezzo Cammin Women Poets Timeline Project. Her poetry has previously appeared in *Ruminate, Blue Line,* and *The Poetry Porch*. This is her first book of poetry.

www.ingramcontent.com/pod-product-compliance
Lightning Source LLC
LaVergne TN
LVHW040116080426
835507LV00041B/1095